FUNKY JUNK

Cool stuff to make with hardware

Renée Schwarz

KIDS CAN PRESS

To Sophie, Alex and Pippa, the nuts and bolts of my life

Kids Can Press acknowledges the financial support of the Government of Canada, through the BPIDP, for our publishing activity.

Published in Canada by
Kids Can Press Ltd.
29 Birch Avenue
Toronto, ON M4V 1E2

www.kidscanpress.com

Published in the U.S. by
Kids Can Press Ltd.
2250 Military Road
Tonawanda, NY 14150

Edited by Stacey Roderick
Designed by Karen Powers
Cover photography by Ray Boudreau
Interior photography by Frank Baldassarra
Printed in Hong Kong, China, by
Wing King Tong Company Limited

The hardcover edition of this book is smyth sewn casebound.
The paperback edition of this book is limp sewn with a drawn-on cover.

CM 03 0 9 8 7 6 5 4 3 2 1
CM PA 03 0 9 8 7 6 5 4 3 2 1

National Library of Canada Cataloguing in Publication Data

Schwarz, Renée
    Funky junk : cool stuff to make with hardware / Renée Schwarz.

(Kids can do it)

ISBN 1-55337-387-1 (bound).
ISBN 1-55337-388-X (pbk.)

1. Handicraft — Juvenile literature. I. Title. II. Series.

TT160.S35 2003   j745.5   C2002-903079-X

Kids Can Press is a ℓ☉ℾυ𝗌™ Entertainment company

Contents

Introduction

Funky junk is cool little things made with odds and ends you find in a hardware store. The projects in this book are super fast and fun to make — and useful, too. You'll transform everyday things, such as hooks, magnets, zippers and pencil sharpeners, into unique objects. You can even make a chess set from a bunch of nuts, bolts and washers!

Making funky junk is easy, even if you've never used tools and hardware before and don't know which is the nut and which is the bolt! The instructions tell you exactly what hardware to use, but try different-sized pieces, too. Be inventive! Use hardware in a totally new and wacky way to make something "nutty."

So what are you waiting for? Funky junk … you can't make just one.

MATERIALS

Most of the materials that you will need are sold in hardware stores. You can also look around your home for extra nuts, bolts, washers, etc., but always ask if you can use things.

▶ Hardware

Hardware stores are organized into different sections.

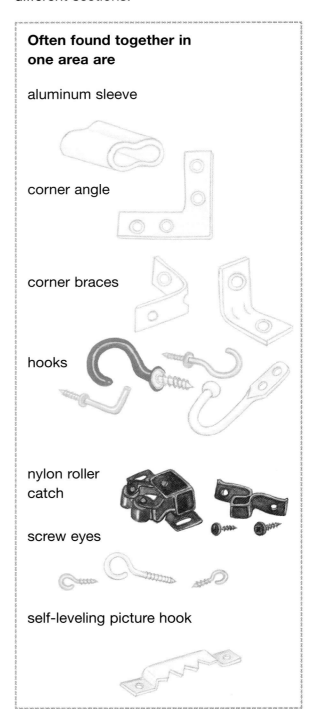

Often found together in one area are

aluminum sleeve

corner angle

corner braces

hooks

nylon roller catch

screw eyes

self-leveling picture hook

In the electrical and automotive sections, you will find

stranded automotive
or electrical wire

squeeze connector

screw connector

spade and ring terminals

springs and expansion
springs

wire connectors

wire rope clip

Grouped together in the hardware section are

screw
anchors

nails

round head and brass
wood screws

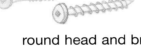

zinc plate washers

locknuts

cap nuts

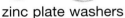

nuts and bolts

wing nut

★ *Nuts and bolts have numbers that
tell you which will screw together. For
example, a ⁶/₃₂ nut will screw onto any
length of ⁶/₃₂ bolt.*

In the plumbing section, you will find

black and white
flat rubber washers

black and white beveled
rubber washers

brass compression
sleeves

▷ Tools

Different tools work with different hardware pieces.

Hammer and nails
Use a hammer and nail to make starter holes for screw eyes or to pierce holes in metal.

Needlenose pliers
Use needlenose pliers for holding, shaping and twisting wire. They can also cut thin wire.

Screwdrivers
The slot on the head of a screw or bolt determines which type and size of screwdriver to use. The tip of the screwdriver should fit tightly enough so that it does not slip out when turned.

Locking pliers and adjustable wrenches
Locking pliers snap closed around the nut and hold it tight so it won't move when you are screwing on the bolt. If you don't have locking pliers, you can use an adjustable wrench instead.

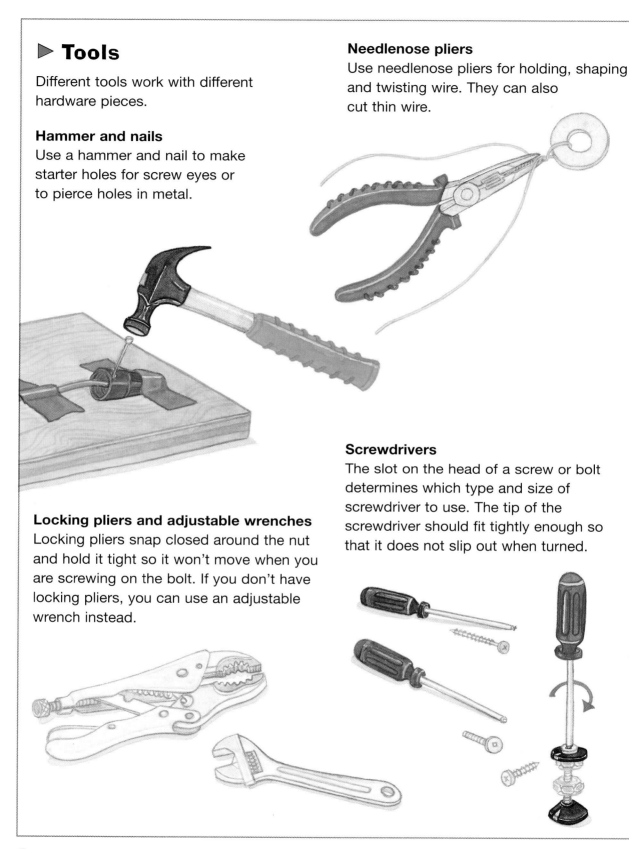

Wire and wire cutters

Thin wire (20 gauge) is used in many projects. It is available in brass, galvanized steel or copper. Stranded automotive or electrical wire is also used. Stranded wire has many very fine copper wires covered in a plastic coating that can be stripped or peeled off.

▶ Glues and tapes

Some projects require white glue. Others require a strong glue recommended for metal or an epoxy. Epoxy is available in either putty form, which is easy to work with, or as 5-minute epoxy, which dries very quickly. Ask an adult to help when using an epoxy, and follow the manufacturer's instructions.

Use wire cutters to cut wire. For 20 gauge wire and pipe cleaners, you can also use old nail clippers. Cutting wire or pipe cleaners with scissors will ruin the scissors.

For some projects you will need double-sided mounting tape or electrical tape.

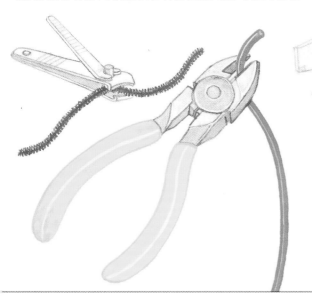

Safety note:

Cut wire is sharp! Wear safety goggles when working with wire.

▶ Craft supplies

You will need tiny roly eyes, beads, feathers, key rings, magnets, pipe cleaners, pins and double metal paint cups. To add color, use either acrylic paint or permanent markers.

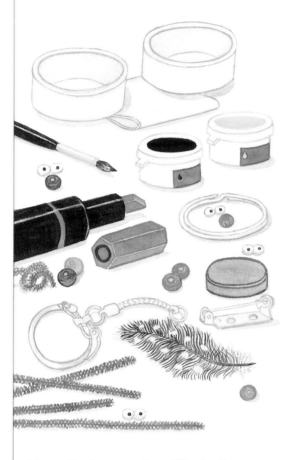

You will also need a utility knife to cut through plastic. Always ask an adult for help when using one.

Tips and techniques

Safety

Wear safety glasses or goggles, especially when working with wire. Cut wire ends can be sharp and can scratch. Never force tools — they could slip and hurt you. If something is too difficult to do, ask an adult for help.

Protecting a work surface

Always protect your work surface. A thick plastic placemat or heavy cardboard can be used, but a wooden board is best when hammering.

Screwing and unscrewing

Screws, nuts and bolts always turn clockwise (to the right) to tighten and counterclockwise (to the left) to loosen. After making a few projects, you will automatically know which way to turn. Just remember: "lefty-loosey, righty-tighty."

Gluing nuts to bolts

If you want a regular nut to stay in place, glue it on. Use a toothpick to dab some white glue on the threads of the bolt, then screw on the nut. Let dry.

Using locknuts

A locknut is a nut with an extra section that locks it in place. To screw a bolt into one, grasp the nut with locking pliers. Screw in the bolt with a screwdriver. Place your hand as shown, so that if the screwdriver slips, you don't stab yourself. Since locknuts can be hard to screw on, you may need to ask an adult for help.

Working with wire and pipe cleaners

Wire ends and cut pipe cleaners can be sharp. Use needlenose pliers to bend the wire end back and squeeze it flat. To curl wire, wind it tightly around a pencil or screwdriver.

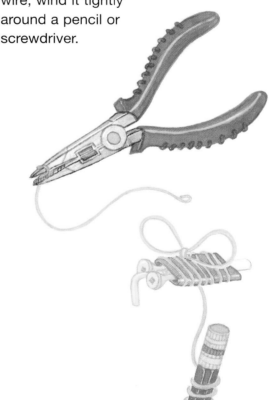

Lock-nest monster

Spot the monster and you'll know you're at the right locker.

You will need

- a ⁷⁄₈ in. red hook
- a combination lock
- a small wooden bead
- a yellow screw anchor
- two tiny roly eyes
- electrical tape, locking pliers, scissors or utility knife, a ruler, strong glue or 5-minute epoxy, a toothpick, a damp rag

1 Wrap a few layers of tape around the jaws of the pliers to cover the teeth or grooves. This protects the plastic coating on the hook.

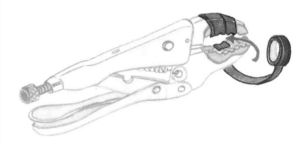

2 Place the hook in the pliers as shown. Gently squeeze the pliers to bend the hook slightly closed.

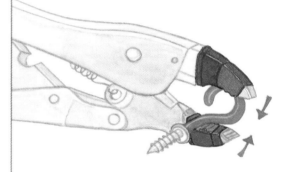

3 Slip an open combination lock through the hook to check that the hook won't fall off. Remove the hook from the lock.

4 For the tail, ask an adult to use scissors or a utility knife to cut the plastic coating off the tip of the hook, 0.5 cm (¼ in.) from the end.

7 Glue the roly eyes onto the screw anchor. Let dry.

5 Glue the bead to the tip of the hook. Let dry.

8 Slip the lock-nest monster onto your lock.

6 Use a toothpick to dab a bit of glue on the threads of the hook's screw. Screw the hook into the screw anchor. Wipe off the excess glue.

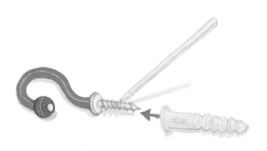

Other ideas

• For a striped monster, wrap thin wire around the hook.

Nutty mouse pin

Make many metal mice.

You will need

- a ¼ wing nut
- a yellow screw anchor
- a ring terminal, 16-14 wire #8-10 stud
- a ¼ locknut
- a ¼ - 20 nut
- a #6 x ¾ in. round head screw
- two tiny roly eyes
- a small metal pin
- needlenose pliers, locking pliers, a screwdriver, strong glue or 5-minute epoxy

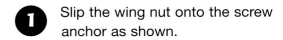

1 Slip the wing nut onto the screw anchor as shown.

2 Slide the ring terminal onto the screw anchor, up to the wing nut.

3 Grasp the plastic coating of the ring terminal with the needlenose pliers. Pull it off by gently turning it. You may need to ask an adult for help.

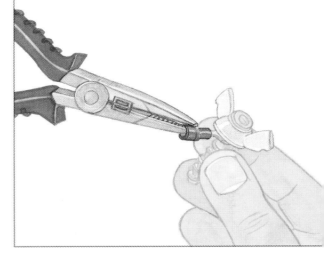

4 Slip the locknut and then the nut onto the screw anchor as shown.

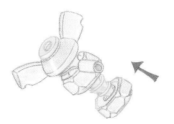

7 Glue the pin to the back of the nuts. Let dry.

5 Holding the locknut with the locking pliers, use the screwdriver to screw the round head screw into the screw anchor.

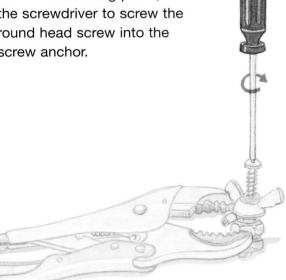

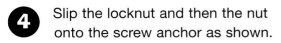

Other ideas

● Instead of using nuts for the body in step 4, wind a pipe cleaner around the screw anchor.

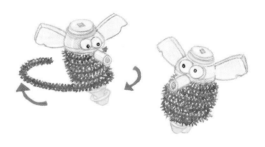

● Glue the mouse to a keychain instead of a pin.

6 Glue the roly eyes onto the wing nut. Let dry.

Zipping snake

A silly snake made in a zippy jiffy. Ssssuper.

You will need

- a 16 cm (6½ in.) length of red 12 gauge or 14 gauge stranded wire
- a blue wire connector
- two small brass screw eyes
- two tiny roly eyes
- a zippered pencil case
- a ruler, wire cutters, a wire stripper or utility knife, electrical tape, a hammer and a small finishing nail, needlenose pliers, a pencil, strong glue or epoxy putty

1 Ask an adult to strip 1 cm (½ in.) of the plastic coating from one end of the stranded wire using a wire stripper or utility knife.

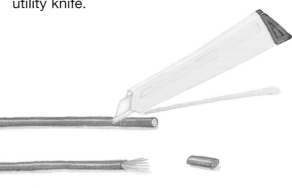

2 Insert the stripped end into the wire connector. Screw the connector on tightly.

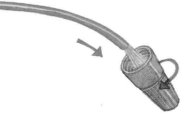

3 Tape the wire and the tip of the connector to your work surface as shown.

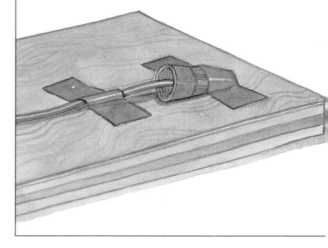

4 Near the rim of the connector, hammer in the nail to make a hole for a screw eye. Pull out the nail and make a second hole about 0.25 cm (⅛ in.) from the first. Pull out the nail. Remove the tape.

7 Glue the roly eyes onto the screw eyes. Let dry.

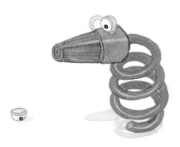

5 Hold a screw eye with the pliers and screw it into one of the holes by turning the connector counterclockwise. Repeat with the other screw eye.

8 Slip the snake through the hole in the pencil case zipper's tab. Tuck in the end of the wire. If tab hole is too small, attach the snake with a small wire ring.

6 Wind the wire around a pencil to curl it. Slip the snake off the pencil.

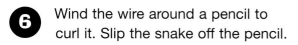

Other ideas

● Slip the snake on a string, attach it to a key ring or use it to decorate your pencil.

Lighting bee switchplate

Light up your life with this sparkling bee.

You will need

- two ⁷⁄₁₆ zinc plate washers
- a 1.2 m (4 ft.) length of 20 gauge brass wire
- two small colored wooden beads
- a light switchplate
- yellow and red reflective safety or automotive tape
- double-sided mounting tape, a pencil, scissors, needlenose pliers, a screwdriver

1 Place the washers on the double-sided tape and trace around them. Cut out the circles and set them aside.

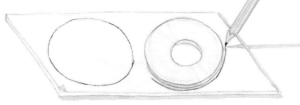

2 Bend the wire in half and slide one washer onto one strand, up to the bend. Use the pliers to grasp the wire around the washer as shown. With your free hand, turn the washer two times to twist the wire.

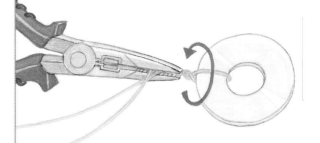

3 Thread one wire strand through the other washer. Slide the washer down beside the first one and wind the wire strand twice around the twisted wire to hold the washer in place.

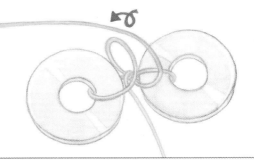

4 For the antennae, wind one wire strand tightly around the screwdriver shank. Slip out the screwdriver. Repeat with the other strand.

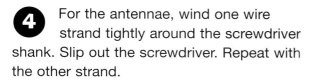
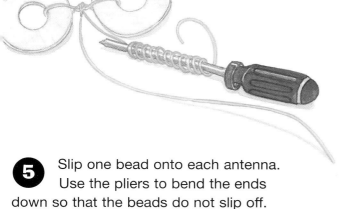

5 Slip one bead onto each antenna. Use the pliers to bend the ends down so that the beads do not slip off.

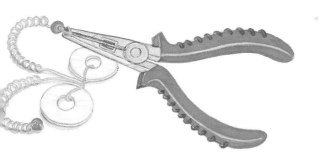

6 Stick a double-sided tape circle to the back of each washer. Stick the washers to the light switchplate.

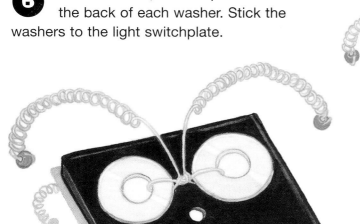

7 Cut dots and stripes out of the reflective tape and decorate the switchplate. Stick dots inside the washer eyes.

8 Ask an adult to install your lighting bee.

Bungee bug bracelet

A wacky friendship bracelet.

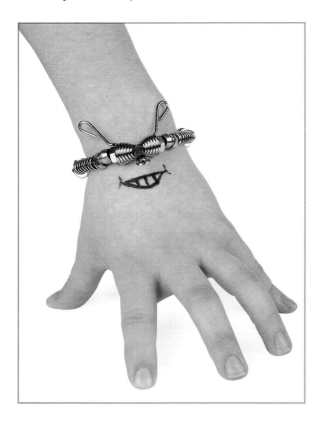

You will need

- a blue spade terminal, 16-14 wire #8-10 stud
- a small bungee cord, 25 cm (10 in.) long
- a ¾ in. screw eye
- two springs, about ⁵⁄₁₆ in. x 1¾ in.
- locknuts: two ¹⁰⁄₂₄, two ¼
- two ¼ in. brass compression sleeves
- nuts: six ¹⁰⁄₂₄, two ¼
- needlenose pliers, scissors and matches, wire cutters

1 Grasp the spade terminal with the tip of the pliers. Bend the blue tube around the tip of the pliers as shown, so that the metal prongs form a hook.

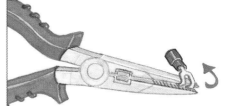

2 For the nose, hook the spade terminal around the middle of the bungee cord. Use the pliers to squeeze the prongs tight to hold it in place.

3 Screw the screw eye into the spade terminal.

4 Slide the bungee hooks to the center of the cord. Use the pliers to grasp the hooks near the coiled part and bend them up a bit. You may need to ask an adult for help.

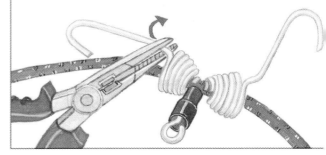

18

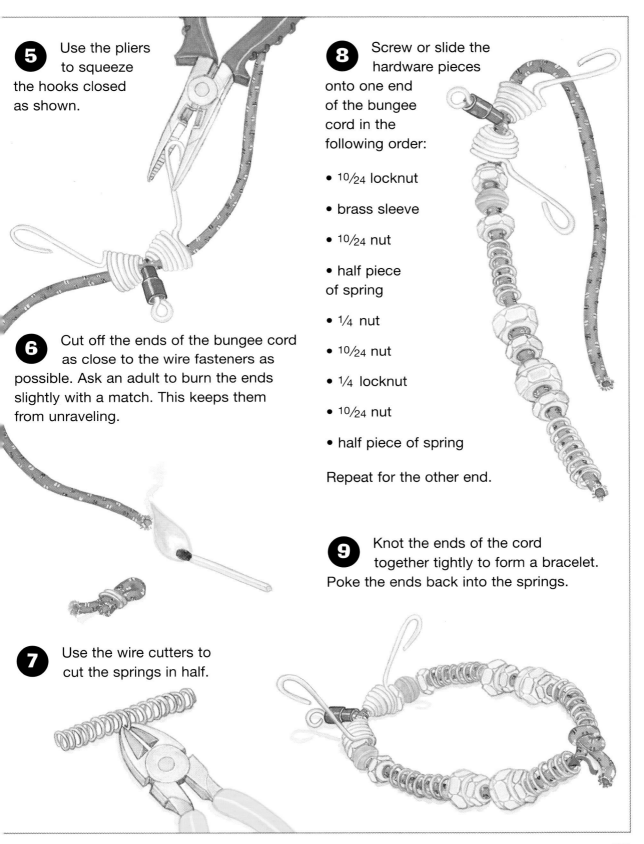

5 Use the pliers to squeeze the hooks closed as shown.

6 Cut off the ends of the bungee cord as close to the wire fasteners as possible. Ask an adult to burn the ends slightly with a match. This keeps them from unraveling.

7 Use the wire cutters to cut the springs in half.

8 Screw or slide the hardware pieces onto one end of the bungee cord in the following order:

- $10/24$ locknut

- brass sleeve

- $10/24$ nut

- half piece of spring

- $1/4$ nut

- $10/24$ nut

- $1/4$ locknut

- $10/24$ nut

- half piece of spring

Repeat for the other end.

9 Knot the ends of the cord together tightly to form a bracelet. Poke the ends back into the springs.

Critter clip

Clip this critter to a notebook or binder to keep your pencils and papers handy.

You will need

- pipe cleaners: one red, three black, one blue, one metallic blue
- a 3 cm (1¼ in.) wide metal clip
- a small cap nut
- two blue screw anchors
- a small plate washer
- a small nut
- wire cutters, a pencil, strong glue or 5-minute epoxy, a ruler

1 For the tongue, cut off one-third of the red pipe cleaner and wind it three times around the tip of one handle of the clip.

2 Make a loop by winding the pipe cleaner around the pencil once. Turn the pencil to tighten the loop, enough to hold the pencil. Slide out the pencil. Wind the rest of the pipe cleaner around the clip's handle.

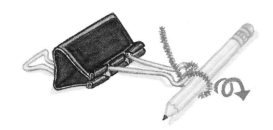

3 For the nose, wind one black pipe cleaner around the end of the handle, covering the red pipe cleaner but not the loop. Glue the cap nut on the tip and let dry.

4 For the snout, wind the blue pipe cleaner up around the rest of the handle. Then wind the metallic blue pipe cleaner over it.

5 For the ears, break the little piece inside each screw anchor that holds it closed. Roll 8 cm (3 in.) of one black pipe cleaner into a ball. Insert the straight end into one of the screw anchors. Pull it through so that the ball catches in the hole.

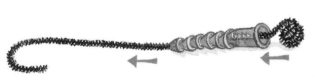

6 Slide the screw anchor onto the clip. Wind the pipe cleaner around the clip once to come out the other side.

7 Poke the end of the pipe cleaner through the pointy side of the other screw anchor. Slip the screw anchor onto the other side of the clip and roll the remaining end of the pipe cleaner into a ball that you stuff in the hole.

8 Wrap the last black pipe cleaner around the top of the clip.

9 For the eyes, glue the washer and the nut to the clip as shown. Let dry.

Baby bird magnet

This baby bird definitely has a magnetic personality.

You will need

- four ³/₁₆ zinc plate washers
- a bronze double nylon roller catch (including two screws)
- four ⁶/₃₂ locknuts
- a 35 cm (14 in.) length of 20 gauge copper wire
- a round magnet, 2 cm (¾ in.) diameter
- a feather
- locking pliers, needlenose pliers, wire cutters, double-sided tape or strong glue, a screwdriver

1 For one eye, slip a washer onto one of the roller catch screws and then put the screw through a hole on the triangular striker (the bird's head).

2 Add another washer to the screw and screw on a locknut (see page 9). Then screw on a second locknut.

3 Repeat steps 1 and 2 for the other eye.

4 Bend the wire in half and poke it up through the square part of the roller catch (the bird's body). The wire ends should pass through on either side of the spring. Pull the ends so that the wire hooks on the spring.

5 Poke the needlenose pliers in the hole and grab both wires. Use your free hand to turn the body, twisting the wires together to about 1.5 cm (⅝ in.) outside the hole.

7 Wind the ends of the wire around the neck (the twisted length of wire). Poke the ends into the hole in the body.

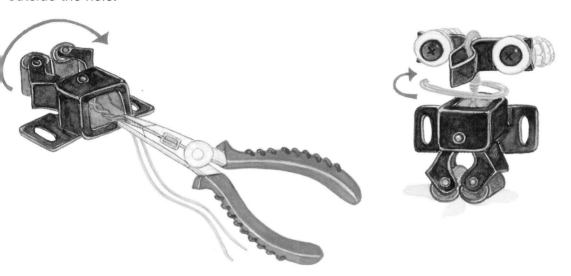

6 To attach the head to the body, place the head on top of the twisted wire. Bend the wire ends down through the beak, then up behind the head and down through the beak again.

8 Use the double-sided tape or glue to stick the magnet to the back of the bird's body and the feather to the back of its head. If you use glue, let dry.

Alien key chain

This little extraterrestrial will keep your keys safe, so you can always go home.

1 For the arms, grasp one end of the wire with the needlenose pliers and bend it to form a small hook. Repeat at the other end.

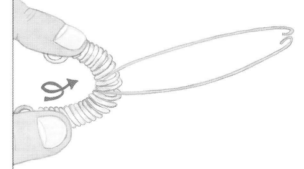

2 Bend the spring to make a gap near the center and slip the middle of the wire through. Wind one wire strand around the spring once, so that the wire is caught in the spring.

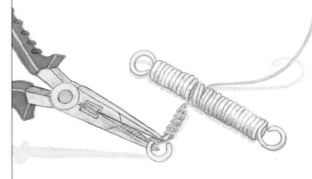

3 Slip a wire hook onto the ring of one screw eye. Use the needlenose pliers to grasp the hook and the ring firmly, then wind the wire tightly around the screw threads, about six times. Repeat for the other arm.

You will need

- a 15 cm (6 in.) length of 20 gauge brass wire
- an expansion spring, 1⅞ in. x 5⁄16 in.
- two ¾ in. screw eyes
- two 3⁄16 in. wire rope clips
- two ¼ - 20 nuts
- two 5⁄16 in. brass compression sleeves
- a key ring
- needlenose pliers, locking pliers, white glue and a toothpick, yellow and black acrylic paint and a small paint brush

4 For the legs, unscrew the nuts from one rope clip and take it apart. Slip the U-bolt from the rope clip through a ring on one end of the spring.

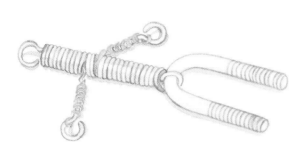

5 Slide the rope clip piece back onto the U-bolt. Use a toothpick to dab a bit of glue on the threads of the bolt.

6 Before the glue dries, screw a nut on a leg to hold the rope clip in place. Slip on a compression sleeve, then tightly screw on another nut. Repeat for the other leg.

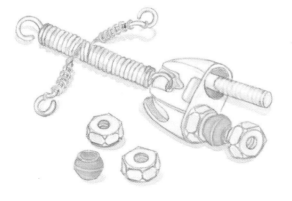

7 For the head, loosen the nuts on the other rope clip. Slip the spring through the opening.

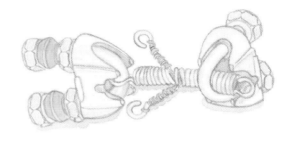

8 Use a toothpick to dab a bit of glue on the threads of the U-bolt as shown. Use the locking pliers to tighten the nuts, so the spring won't pull out. Let dry.

9 Slip the key ring through the spring ring. Paint yellow eyes with tiny black dots for pupils on the ends of the U-bolt. Let dry.

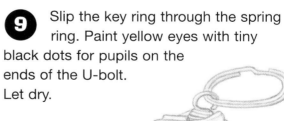

Fat fly pencil pal

Wind a fat fly around a pencil and let your imagination buzz.

You will need

- two #4 x ⅝ in. brass wood screws
- a 7/16 in. or 9/16 in. brass hook
- a thin eraser stick, about 2.5 cm x 0.25 cm (1 in. x ⅛ in.)
- a 40 cm (16 in.) length of 20 gauge brass wire
- pipe cleaners: one metallic blue, one metallic red
- electrical tape, a pencil, wire cutters, a thick marker, a ruler and needlenose pliers

1 Use a small piece of tape to hold the screws on either side of the hook as shown.

2 Tape the eraser to the hook and screws. This is the body.

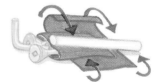

3 For the wings, wrap the middle of the wire around a marker and twist it twice to hold the loop. Slide the marker out.

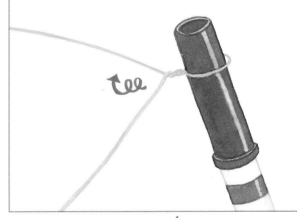

4 Repeat to form a second loop. The loops should form an "8."

7 Wind the blue pipe cleaner tightly around the front half of the body and once behind the wings. Squeeze the end down so it does not unravel.

5 Wind one wire strand around the body as shown.

8 Cut the red pipe cleaner in half and wind one piece tightly around the back end, leaving about 0.5 cm (¼ in.) of the eraser uncovered. Wind it once in front of the wings. Squeeze the end down.

6 Wind the other strand tightly around a pencil, stopping about 2.5 cm (1 in.) from the fly. Slide the pencil out carefully.

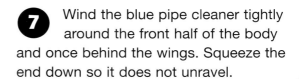

Other ideas

● Cut off the second strand (step 6) and glue your fly to a metal pin.

Sharpie the robot

Command this robot to keep your pencils sharp.

You will need

- a small metal pencil sharpener
- a ½ in. squeeze connector
- a 115 cm (46 in.) length of 20 gauge galvanized steel wire
- a U-bolt from a 5/16 in. wire rope clip
- a ¾ in. 2-screw connector
- two 5/16 locknuts
- two blue spade terminals
- two 10/24 locknuts
- a 60 cm (24 in.) length of 20 gauge copper wire
- two tiny roly eyes
- strong glue or epoxy putty, a screwdriver, wire cutters, a ruler, needlenose pliers, locking pliers, a red permanent marker

1 For the head, glue the pencil sharpener into the squeeze connector so that the narrow end of the sharpener sticks out just past the ring. Tighten the "nose" bolt slightly with a screwdriver.

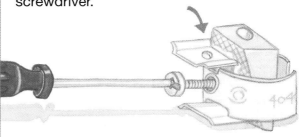

2 Cut a 40 cm (16 in.) length of galvanized wire and wrap it around the ring four times — twice above the nose and twice below. Use the needlenose pliers to twist the ends tightly together twice at the back and cut off the extra wire.

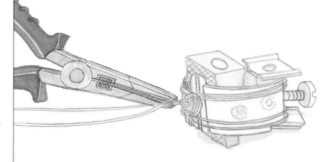

3 Tighten the nose bolt with a screwdriver. Let the glue you applied in step 1 dry.

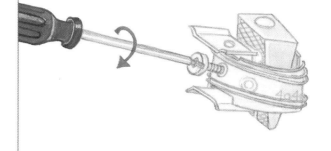

4 For the legs, insert the U-bolt into the 2-screw connector until the top of the U-bolt threads are even with the bottom of the connector. Use the screwdriver to tighten the connector bolts to hold the U-bolt in place.

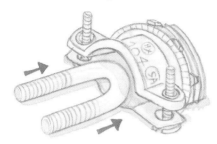

5 Screw a ⁵⁄₁₆ locknut onto each leg of the U-bolt (see page 9), then unscrew them. This should make grooves in the nylon part of the U-bolt.

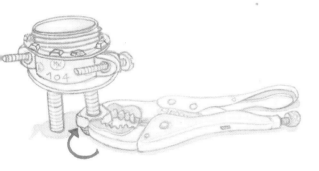

6 Reverse the locknuts so the round side is up, and screw them back onto the U-bolt. The bottoms of the nuts should be even with the ends of the bolt.

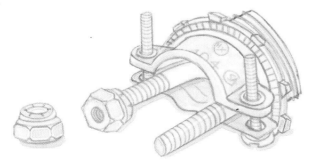

7 For one arm, cut a 15 cm (6 in.) length of galvanized wire. Bend the wire in half and hook it onto an "arm" bolt of the 2-screw connector. Wind the wire around the bolt twice.

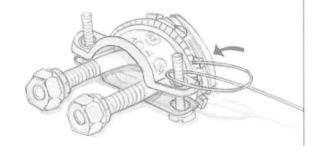

8 Poke the wire ends through a spade terminal. Wind them around the "wrist" twice. Cut off the extra wire.

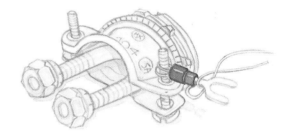

9 Screw a ¹⁰⁄₂₄ locknut onto the arm bolt. Repeat steps 7 to 9 for the second arm.

10 Bend the copper wire in half. Poke the ends through the hole on top of the head so that the wire passes on either side of the nose bolt and comes out the bottom hole. Pull the wire until the bend catches onto the nose bolt.

13 To attach the head to the body, poke the copper wire ends down through the body, in front of the U-bolt. Then poke the galvanized wire ends up through the head, on each side of the sharpener.

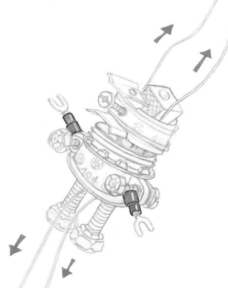

11 Cut a 45 cm (18 in.) length of galvanized wire and bend it in half. Poke the ends up the body between the legs and out the neck so that the bend hooks onto the U-bolt.

14 Pull on both the copper wire and the galvanized wire ends until the head touches the body.

12 Poke one wire end down back through the body and up again to wrap the wire around the U-bolt once.

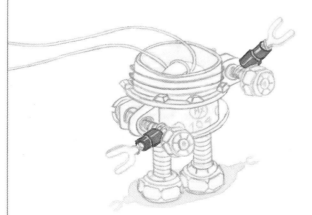

15 Holding the head firmly on top of the body, wind one copper wire tightly around each leg.

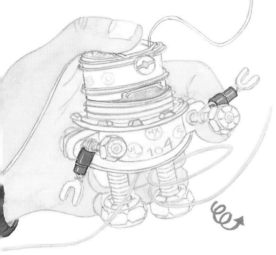

16 Still holding the head firmly in place, cross the galvanized wires over the top of the head. Poke them down through the head and out the bottom of the body.

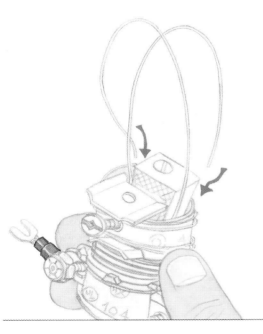

17 Use the needlenose pliers to reach into the body and grab the two galvanized wires just below the U-bolt. Holding the wires tightly, turn the body a few times to twist them together. Cut off the extra wire and poke up the ends to hide them in the body.

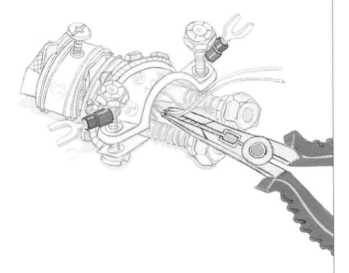

18 Color the squares of the collar ring with the marker. Glue on the roly eyes. Let dry.

Guard dog hook

No one would dare take your keys from this ferocious beast.

You will need

- a set of double metal paint cups, 4 cm (1½ in.) diameter
- an aluminum sleeve, 3/16 in. x 1 in.
- a scrap of wood, at least 1 cm (½ in.) thick
- a ¾ in. metal hook
- a white plastic bottle cap, about 2.5 cm (1 in.) diameter
- a self-leveling picture hook
- black rubber plumbing washers: one beveled 3/8 L (11/16 in.), one flat 3/8 L (11/16 in.)
- bolts: one 8/32 x 2 in., two 6/32 x ½ in., one ¼ x ½ in., one 10/24 x ½ in.
- nuts: one 8/32, one 3/8 - 16, one ¼
- locknuts: two 8/32, one ¼, one 10/24
- six 6/32 cap nuts (for hook)
- zinc plate washers: two 3/16, three 3/8
- a 25 mm (1 in.) inside corner brace
- two 38 mm (1½ in.) flat corner angles
- string, about 20 cm (8 in.)
- a hammer and a 2 in. nail, a utility knife, needlenose pliers, screwdriver, locking pliers, strong glue or 5-minute epoxy

1 For the head, unbend the metal clip part of the paint cups.

2 To mark the hole for the snout on the paint clip, place the aluminum sleeve between the paint cups as shown. Put the nail through the top hole of the sleeve and hammer lightly. Be sure to be precise. Remove the nail and sleeve.

3 Turn the paint cups over and hold the metal clip part up with the scrap of wood. Hammer the nail through the clip at the mark you made in step 2. Pull the nail out.

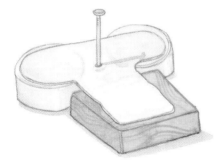

4 Repeat steps 2 and 3 to make as many holes as needed for the hook.

5 Use the hammer and nail to make a hole near the top of the bottle cap. Before pulling the nail out, wiggle the nail in the hole to make it slightly bigger.

6 For the teeth, ask an adult to cut two slits in the bottle cap with a utility knife as shown.

7 Use the needlenose pliers to bend both ends of the picture hook down. Insert the bent ends through the slits in the bottle cap, "teeth" pointing up. Use the pliers to bend the ends more, so they are flat against the inside top of the cap.

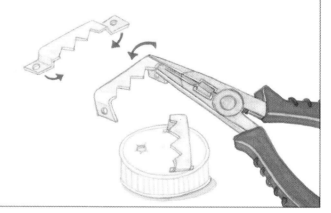

8 For the nose, screw the black beveled washer onto the 2 in. bolt. Then screw the bolt through the hole in the bottle cap and screw on an 8/32 nut.

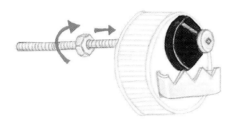

9 Slip the aluminum sleeve onto the bolt. Poke the end of the bolt through the hole in the paint clip you made in step 2. Screw on an 8/32 locknut to hold the bolt in place (see page 9). Screw on the other 8/32 locknut so that it is even with the end of the bolt.

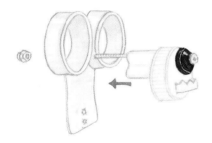

10 Put a 3/16 zinc washer onto each 6/32 x 1/2 in. bolt. From the back, put the bolts through the hole(s) you made for the hook in step 4.

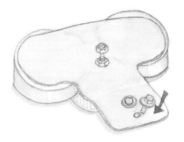

11 Put on the hook, then use locking pliers to tightly screw a cap nut onto each bolt.

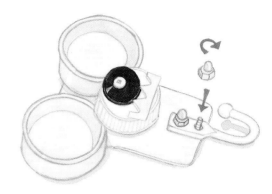

12 Glue on the remaining cap nuts to form the studded collar as shown. Let dry.

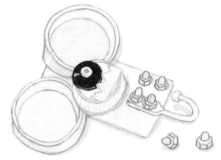

13 For one eye, slip the 3/8 nut onto the 1/4 bolt. Use the locking pliers and screwdriver to screw on the 1/4 locknut.

14 Glue a 3/8 zinc washer in one paint cup. Glue the end of the locknut from step 13 into the washer's hole. Let dry.

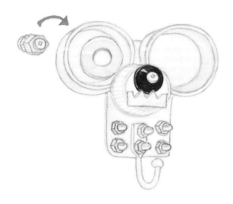

15 For the other eye, slip the 1/4 nut onto the 10/24 bolt. Screw on the black flat washer, then use the locking pliers and a screwdriver to screw on the 10/24 locknut.

16 Glue two 3/8 zinc washers, one on top of the other, in the other paint cup. Glue the end of the locknut from step 15 into the washers' hole. Let dry.

17 For the eyebrows, glue the corner brace between the paint cups. Let dry.

18 For the ears, glue the flat corner angles to the back as shown. Let dry.

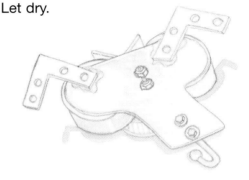

19 Tie a string around the ears and hang up your guard dog.

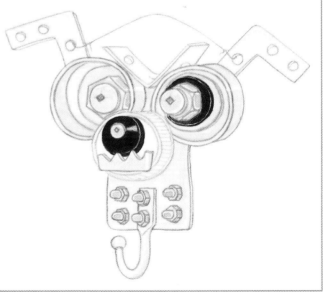

35

Heavy metal chess set

For someone who is nuts about chess.

▶ Hardware you will need

Pawn

- a ¼ x 1 in. round head bolt
- nuts: two ¼-20
- plumbing washers: one flat ¼ L (19⁄32 in.), one beveled 3⁄8 R (5⁄8 in.) or 3⁄8 L (11⁄16 in.)

Note: *You will need to enlarge the holes of the plumbing washers a bit. Ask an adult to scrape the inside with a utility knife until the tip of the bolt just fits in.*

Castle

- a 10⁄32 x 1½ in. round head bolt
- nuts: one 5⁄16-18, one 3⁄8-16, one 7⁄16-14
- plumbing washers: one flat ¼ M (0) (17⁄32 in.), one flat ¼ L (19⁄32 in.), one flat 3⁄8 L (11⁄16 in.), one beveled 3⁄8 L (11⁄16 in.)

Knight

- a 6⁄32 x 1½ in. flat head bolt
- a ¼ in. wing nut
- nuts: three 6⁄32, two 8⁄32
- a ¼ locknut
- a 10⁄32 cap nut
- plumbing washers: one flat ¼ M (0) (17⁄32 in.), one beveled 3⁄8 L (11⁄16 in.)
- zinc plate washers: two 3⁄16
- a metal ring terminal: 22-16 or 22-18

Bishop

- an 8⁄32 x 1½ in. round head bolt
- nuts: one ¼-20, three 8⁄32, one 3⁄8-16
- plumbing washers: one flat ¼ R (9⁄16 in.), one flat ¼ L (19⁄32 in.), one beveled 3⁄8 L (11⁄16 in.)
- a 5⁄16 zinc plate washer

King

- a 10⁄24 x 2½ in. flat head bolt
- a 10⁄24 wing nut
- nuts: one 5⁄16, three 10⁄24, one 3⁄8
- a ¼ locknut
- plumbing washers: one flat ¼ L (19⁄32 in.), one flat 3⁄8 L (11⁄16 in.), one beveled ½ R (3⁄4 in.)
- zinc plate washers: one 3⁄8, one 5⁄16, one ¼

Queen

- a 10⁄24 x 2 in. round head bolt
- nuts: three 10⁄24, one ¼
- a 10⁄24 locknut
- plumbing washers: one flat ¼ L (19⁄32 in.), one beveled 3⁄8 L (11⁄16 in.), one flat ½ R (3⁄4 in.)
- zinc plate washers: two 3⁄8, one ¼, one 3⁄16, one 5⁄16, two 7⁄16
- a 50 cm (20 in.) length of 20 gauge brass wire

▶ Tools you will need

- a utility knife
- white glue and toothpicks
- screwdrivers (to fit the various bolts)
- a ruler
- locking pliers
- strong glue or epoxy putty
- a damp rag
- a wrench

A complete chess set has 16 black pieces and 16 white pieces. Make one set of the following using black plumbing washers and another set using white washers: one king, one queen, two bishops, two knights, two castles and eight pawns.

▶ Tip

When buying supplies, keep the hardware for each chess piece in separate bags. It can be difficult to tell some of the hardware pieces apart!

Pawn

1 Place the flat washer on your work surface. Put the bolt in the hole. Holding the washer firmly so it does not turn, screw in the bolt using the screwdriver. Then hold the washer tightly in your hand and continue screwing until the bolt pokes out past the washer.

2 Screw a nut onto the end of the bolt. Grasp the nut with the locking pliers and use the screwdriver to screw in the bolt. The nut will push the washer up to the top.

3 Screw on the second nut by hand until it is about about 0.5 cm (¼ in.) from the end. Glue it in place. Let dry.

4 Place the beveled washer on your work surface. Holding the washer firmly so it does not turn, screw in the bolt using the screwdriver, until the end is almost even with the washer.

Castle

1 Screw or slide the hardware pieces onto the bolt in the following order:

- flat ¼ M washer
- ⁵⁄₁₆ nut
- flat ¼ L washer
- ³⁄₈ nut
- flat ³⁄₈ L washer
- ⁷⁄₁₆ nut

2 Fill the space inside the ⁷⁄₁₆ nut with epoxy putty.

3 Coat the threads at the end of the bolt with epoxy putty and screw on the beveled washer base. Fill the hole at the bottom with putty.
Wipe the bottom surface clean.
Let dry.

Knight

1 Screw or slide the hardware pieces onto the bolt in the following order:

- ¼ in. wing nut
- flat ¼ M washer
- ring terminal
- ³⁄₁₆ zinc washer
- ⁶⁄₃₂ nut
- ⁶⁄₃₂ nut
- ⁸⁄₃₂ nut
- ⁸⁄₃₂ nut
- ¼ locknut
- ³⁄₁₆ zinc washer
- ⁶⁄₃₂ nut (tighten with wrench and screwdriver)

2 For the snout, squish a bit of putty into the ¹⁰⁄₃₂ cap nut and slip it onto the ring terminal. Wipe off the excess putty.

3 Repeat step 3 of the castle instructions using the beveled washer.

38

Bishop

1 Screw or slide the hardware pieces onto the bolt in the following order:

- flat 1/4 R washer
- 5/16 zinc washer
- 1/4 nut
- 8/32 nut (tighten with wrench and screwdriver)

Leave a 0.25 cm (1/8 in.) space. Then add

- 8/32 nut
- flat 1/4 L washer
- 3/8 nut
- 8/32 nut (tighten with wrench and screwdriver)

2 Repeat step 3 of the castle instructions using the beveled washer.

King

1 Screw or slide the hardware pieces onto the bolt in the following order:

- 10/24 wing nut
- flat 1/4 L washer
- 3/8 zinc washer
- 5/16 nut
- 5/16 zinc washer
- 10/24 nut (tighten with wrench and screwdriver)

Leave a 0.5 cm (1/4 in.) space. Then add

- 10/24 nut
- 1/4 locknut
- 1/4 zinc washer
- 3/8 nut
- flat 3/8 L washer
- 10/24 nut (tighten with wrench and screwdriver)

2 Repeat step 3 of the castle instructions using the beveled washer.

Queen

1 For the crown, wind the brass wire tightly through the center and around one ⅜ zinc washer, about 25 times.

2 Screw or slide the hardware pieces onto the bolt in the following order:

- flat ¼ L washer
- crown (from step 1)
- ¹⁰/₂₄ nut
- ¼ nut
- ¼ zinc washer
- ¹⁰/₂₄ nut (tighten with wrench and screwdriver)

Leave a 0.5 cm (¼ in.) space. Then add

- ¹⁰/₂₄ locknut
- ³/₁₆ zinc washer
- beveled ⅜ L washer
- ⁵/₁₆ zinc washer
- ⅜ zinc washer
- ¹⁰/₂₄ nut
- ⁷/₁₆ zinc washer (to fit over the ¹⁰/₂₄ nut)
- ⁷/₁₆ zinc washer

3 Repeat step 3 of the castle instructions using the flat ½ R washer.

▶ **Tip**

To make sure the nuts don't come loose, use a toothpick to dab white glue on the threads of the bolt before screwing the nuts on.

Other ideas

- To make a chess board, use a 25 cm (10 in.) square x 2 cm (¾ in.) thick plank of wood or a heavy piece of cardboard. Draw a 1 cm (½ in.) border all around with a black permanent marker. With a pencil, divide the board into squares by drawing seven lines across and seven lines down, spaced 2.9 cm (1⅛ in.) apart. Color a checkerboard pattern in with the marker.